Step by Step Guide

Anna School Learning

SUMMER MATH WORKBOOK

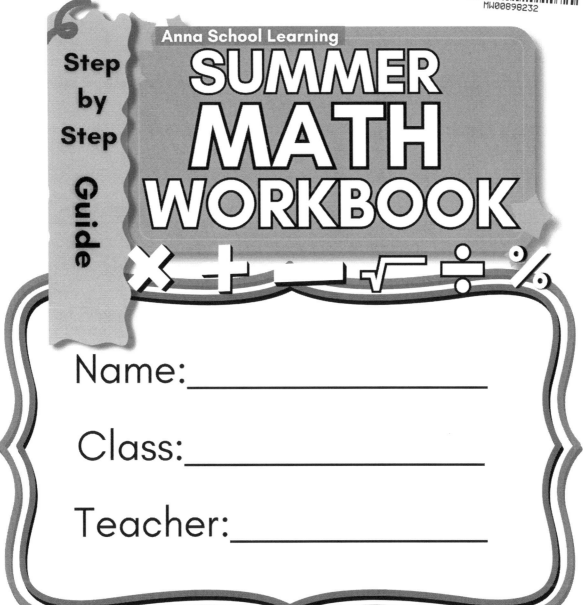

Name:_____

Class:_____

Teacher:_____

Contents

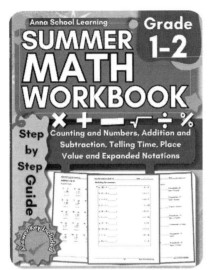

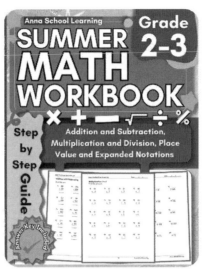

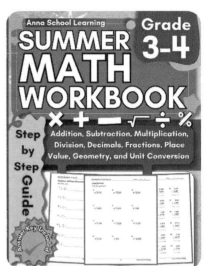

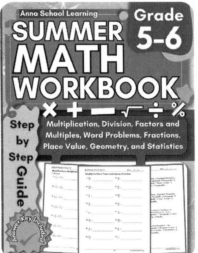

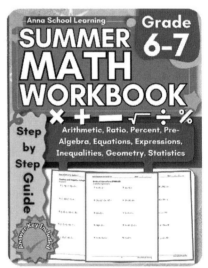

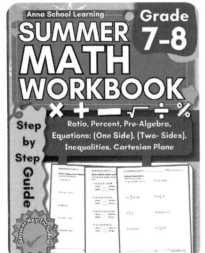

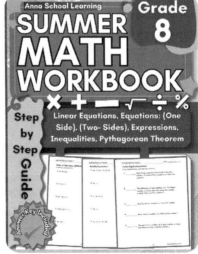

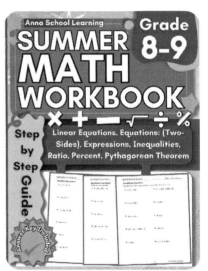

Positive and Negative Integers

Positive and negative integers are whole numbers that can represent quantities greater than zero and less than zero, respectively.

Positive Integers: Positive integers are whole numbers greater than zero. They are denoted by the numbers 1,2,3,4...

Negative Integers: Negative integers are whole numbers less than zero. They are denoted by placing a negative sign ("-") before the numbers, such as -1,-2,-3,-4,...

The positive integers are used to represent the number of objects, scores, etc. whereas the negative integers can be used to represent debt, losses, temperatures below freezing points, etc.

Let's solve some problems:

1. $6 - (-8) - 9$

- Start by simplifying within the parentheses:

$$-(-8) \text{ becomes } 8.$$

- Rewrite the expression with the simplified part:

$$6 + 8 - 9.$$

- Now perform addition and subtraction from left to right:

$$6 + 8 = 14, \text{ then } 14 - 9 = 5$$

2. $(-5) - (-3) + 10$

$$(-5) + 3 + 10$$

$$(-5) + 3 = -2, \text{ then } -2 + 10 = 8$$

Positive and Negative Integers

Evaluate.

1) $(-4) - (-10) + 5 =$

2) $(-10) + (-1) + 6 =$

3) $(-8) + (-10) + (-8) =$

4) $(-2) + (-10) - 7 =$

5) $(-2) + (-9) + 1 =$

6) $4 + (-7) =$

7) $6 - 8 - 5 =$

8) $(-7) + (-8) - 8 =$

9) $(-8) + (-6) + (-8) =$

10) $5 + (-6) + 10 =$

11) $9 - 4 - 8 =$

12) $8 - 7 + 4 =$

13) $3 + 10 - 6 =$

14) $(-6) + (-4) =$

15) $(-6) - 10 + (-2) =$

16) $4 - 2 + 9 =$

17) $(-4) - 8 =$

18) $5 + 3 - 2 =$

19) $(-3) + (-8) - 8 =$

20) $(-3) + 6 =$

21) $3 - 8 + 4 =$

22) $3 + 1 - 2 =$

23) $10 + (- 10) =$

24) $9 - 3 + 10 =$

25) $5 + 6 - 9 =$

26) $4 - 1 + 1 =$

27) $(-4) - (-10) + 7 =$

28) $7 - 4 + 6 =$

29) $(-8) + 5 + (-7) =$

30) $(-2) - 8 + (-8) =$

Exponents

An exponent tells you how many times a number (called the base) is multiplied by itself. It is written as a superscript to the right of the base number. For example, in 2^3, 2 is the base and 3 is the exponent.

Rules:

1. **Product Rule**: When multiplying powers with the same base, add the exponents.

$$a^m \times a^n = a^{m+n}$$

For example:

$$2^3 = 2 \times 2 \times 2 = 8$$

$$3^2 \times 3^4 = 3^{2+4} = 3^6 = 3 \times 3 \times 3 \times 3 \times 3 \times 3 = 729$$

2. **Quotient Rule**: When dividing powers with the same base, subtract the exponents.

$$a^m \div a^n = a^{m-n}$$

For example:

$$5^3 \div 5^2 = 5^{3-2} = 5^1 = 5$$

3. **Power of a Power Rule**: When raising a power to another power, multiply the exponents.

$$(a^m)^n = a^{mn}$$

For example:

$$(2^2)^3 = 2^{2 \times 3} = 26 = 64$$

4. **Power of a Product Rule**: When raising a product to a power, distribute the power to each factor.

$$(ab)^n = a^n \times b^n$$

For example:

$$(2 \times 3)^2 = 2^2 \times 3^2 = 4 \times 9 = 36$$

5. **Power of a Quotient Rule**: When raising a quotient to a power, distribute the power to the numerator and denominator separately.

$$\left(\frac{a}{b}\right)^n = \frac{a^n}{b^n}$$

For example:

$$\left(\frac{4}{2}\right)^3 = \frac{4^3}{2^3} = \frac{64}{8} = 8$$

6. **Zero Exponent Rule**: Any nonzero number raised to the power of zero equals 11.

$$a^0 = 1$$

For example:

$$7^0 = 1$$

7. **Negative Exponent Rule**: A negative exponent means the reciprocal of the base raised to the positive exponent.

$$a^{-n} = \frac{1}{a^n}$$

For example:

$$2^{-3} = \frac{1}{2^3} = \frac{1}{8}$$

To evaluate expressions with exponents, we can use:

- **Repeated Multiplication**: Perform the multiplication indicated by the exponent.

- **Using the Rules of Exponents**: Apply the appropriate rule to simplify expressions involving exponents.

Exponents

Convert the values.

1) 13^{-3} = _____

2) 8^{-3} = _____

3) 10^{3} = _____

4) 5^{4} = _____

5) 19^{2} = _____

6) 18^{-2} = _____

7) 14^{-3} = _____

8) 9^{4} = _____

9) 11^{4} = _____

10) 6^{3} = _____

11) 11^{2} = _____

12) 7^{3} = _____

13) $14^4 =$

14) $1^3 =$

15) $1^4 =$

16) $3^{-2} =$

17) $7^4 =$

18) $20^4 =$

19) $10^{-3} =$

20) $6^{-2} =$

21) $9^{-2} =$

22) $18^4 =$

23) $11^3 =$

24) $16^3 =$

Square Roots

The square root of a number is a value that, when multiplied by itself, gives the original number. It's denoted by the symbol √.

For example, the square root of 9 is 3 because 3 * 3 = 9.

Cube Roots

The cube root of a number is a value that, when multiplied by itself twice, gives the original number. It's denoted by the symbol $^3√$.

For example, the cube root of 8 is 2 because 2 * 2 * 2 = 8.

Square and Cube Roots

Calculate the root of each value.

1) $\sqrt[3]{125}$ = _____

2) $\sqrt{16}$ = _____

3) $\sqrt{441}$ = _____

4) $\sqrt{9}$ = _____

5) $\sqrt[3]{27}$ = _____

6) $\sqrt[3]{8}$ = _____

7) $\sqrt[3]{729}$ = _____

8) $\sqrt{9,801}$ = _____

9) $\sqrt{2,809}$ = _____

10) $\sqrt{36}$ = _____

11) $\sqrt{1,936}$ = _____

12) $\sqrt[3]{1}$ = _____

13) $\sqrt{225}$ = _____

14) $\sqrt{100}$ = _____

15) $\sqrt{25}$ = _____

16) $\sqrt[3]{4,913}$ = _____

17) $\sqrt{1}$ = _____

18) $\sqrt[3]{64}$ = _____

19) $\sqrt[3]{8,000}$ = _____

20) $\sqrt[3]{2,744}$ = _____

21) $\sqrt[3]{343}$ = _____

22) $\sqrt[3]{6,859}$ = _____

23) $\sqrt[3]{1,000}$ = _____

24) $\sqrt{900}$ = _____

25) $\sqrt{49}$ = _____

26) $\sqrt{6,561}$ = _____

27) $\sqrt{4}$ = _____

28) $\sqrt[3]{216}$ = _____

29) $\sqrt{961}$ = _____

30) $\sqrt[3]{2,197}$ = _____

Factors

Factors are numbers that divide another number without leaving a remainder.

For example, the factors of 12 are 1, 2, 3, 4, 6, and 12 because these numbers can divide 12 evenly.

Factors always come in pairs, except for perfect squares.

Multiples

Multiples are the result of multiplying a number by an integer.

For example, the multiples of 3 are 3, 6, 9, 12, 15, and so on because these numbers are obtained by multiplying 3 by 1, 2, 3, 4, 5, and so on.

Every number has an infinite number of multiples.

Every factor of a number is a divisor of that number, and every multiple of a number is divisible by that number.

Let's solve some problems:

Factors of 44

2, 4, 11, 22

Multiples of 77

77, 154, 231, 308, 385

Factors

1) 1 _____

2) 47 _____

3) 97 _____

4) 58 _____

5) 44 _____

6) 8 _____

7) 3 _____

8) 46 _____

9) 4 _____

10) 32 _____

11) 89 _____

12) 41 _____

13) 28 _____

14) 98 _____

15) 37 _____

16) 49 _____

17) 15 _____

18) 69 _____

19) 19 _____

20) 5 _____

21) 9 _____

22) 6 _____

23) 78 _____

24) 75 _____

Multiples

1) 20 _____

2) 11 _____

3) 3 _____

4) 2 _____

5) 62 _____

6) 17 _____

7) 25 _____

8) 6 _____

9) 8 _____

10) 9 _____

11) 13 _____

12) 93 _____

13) 7 _____

14) 56 _____

15) 74 _____

16) 19 _____

17) 39 _____

18) 72 _____

19) 27 _____

20) 79 _____

21) 26 _____

22) 64 _____

23) 1 _____

24) 44 _____

Order of Operations (PEMDAS)

The order of operations, often remembered by the acronym PEMDAS, stands for:

- **Parentheses**: Perform operations inside parentheses first.
- **Exponents**: Evaluate exponents (powers and roots) next.
- **Multiplication and Division**: Perform multiplication and division from left to right.
- **Addition and Subtraction**: Perform addition and subtraction from left to right.

The order of operations helps to clarify which operations should be performed first in a mathematical expression to ensure consistent and accurate results.

- **Parentheses**: Evaluate expressions within parentheses first. If there are nested parentheses, start with the innermost ones and work your way out.

  1. Example: $2 \times (3 + 4) = 2 \times 7 = 14$

- **Exponents**: Evaluate expressions with exponents (powers and roots) next.

  1. Example: $2^3 + 4 = 8 + 4 = 12$

- **Multiplication and Division**: Perform multiplication and division from left to right.

  1. Example: $2 \times 3 + 4 = 6 + 4 = 10$

  2. Example: $6 \div 2 \times 3 = 3 \times 3 = 9$

- **Addition and Subtraction**: Perform addition and subtraction from left to right.

  1. Example: $2 + 3 \times 4 = 2 + 12 = 14$

  2. Example: $10 - 4 \div 2 = 10 - 2 = 8$

Order of Operations (PEMDAS)
Evaluate Expressions.

1) $4 + 9 + 2 =$

2) $1(1 + 4) =$

3) $(10 + 5)^2 + (4 + 4)^2 =$

4) $(9 + 10) \div 8 =$

5) $1(6 + 5) =$

6) $7 \times 3 + 5 =$

7) $10(8 + 2) =$

8) $4 + 10 - 2 + 2 =$

9) $3 + 8 + 5 + 4 =$

10) $5 \times 10 =$

11) $6 \times 4 =$

12) $(5 + 9)^2 + (2 + 1)^2 =$

13) $4 \times 7 + 3 =$

14) $(7^2) \times (8^2) + 1 =$

15) $2(2 + 3) =$

16) $(2 \times 1) - (3 + 5) =$

17) $5 \times 6 + 6 =$

18) $5 + 2 - 6 + 3 =$

19) $10 \times 10 \times 1 =$

20) $2 + 10 + 1 =$

21) $10 + 10 - 5 + 4 =$

22) $(7^2) \times (7^2) + 4 =$

23) $(7 \times 9) - (9 + 8) =$

24) $1 + 5 + 4 + 9 =$

25) $(1 \times 9) - (2 + 8) =$

26) $3 \times 10 + 10 =$

27) $(4 + 10) \div 9 =$

28) $3 + 4 + 10 =$

29) $2 + 5 + 6 =$

30) $(1 + 8) \div 7 =$

Solving Equations (One Side)

Solving one-step equations involves performing a single operation to isolate the variable and find its value.

Let's solve an equation step by step: 16 + x = 31

1. **Identify the Goal:**

    The goal is to isolate the variable x on one side of the equation.

2. **Simplify the Equation:** Combine like terms on both sides of the equation, if necessary.

    The equation is already simplified.

3. **Undo Addition or Subtraction:** If there's addition or subtraction involving the variable, undo it by performing the opposite operation on both sides of the equation.

    Since x is being added to 16, we'll undo this operation by subtracting 16 from both sides of the equation:
    $$16 + x - 16 = 31 - 16$$

4. **Isolate the Variable:** Ensure that the variable is alone on one side of the equation.

    $$x = 15$$

5. **Check Your Solution:** Substitute the value of x back into the original equation to verify that it satisfies the equation.

    $$16 + 15 = 31$$

    $$31 = 31$$

The equation is balanced, so the solution.

Solving Equations: (One Side)

Solve the equations for the variable.

1) $19 = x + 4$

2) $19 = 342 \div x$

3) $15 - x = 5$

4) $18 = 20 - x$

5) $30 = x + 19$

6) $7 \times x = 49$

7) $78 \div x = 13$

8) $6 + 12x = 18$

9) $x \div 2 = 9$

10) $x \times 11 = 33$

11) $182 = 13 \times x$

12) $x - 8 = 4$

13) $4 = 76 \div x$

14) $19x + 1 = 153$

15) $11 + x = 29$

16) $16 - x = 11$

17) $19 + 4x = 43$

18) $20 + x = 34$

19) $0 = 35 - 5x$

20) $3 = x \div 12$

21) $6 = 96 \div x$

22) $15 + 5x = 105$

23) $23 = 20x - 17$

24) $19 = 304 \div x$

25) $170 = 9x + 8$

26) $70 = 5 \times x$

27) $3 = 60 \div x$

28) $x \times 4 = 52$

29) $9 = x \div 3$

30) $6 = x - 7$

Evaluate Expressions

Evaluating expressions involves substituting given values for variables in an expression and then performing the indicated operations to find the result.

For example: Let's evaluate $4x - 10$, when $x = 3$:

Step 1: Substitute the given value for the variable:

Replace every occurrence of x in the expression $4x - 10$ with the given value, which is 3:

$$= 4(3) - 10$$

Step 2: Perform the operations:

Perform the indicated operations according to the order of operations (PEMDAS - Parentheses, Exponents, Multiplication and Division, Addition and Subtraction):

$$= 4 \times 3 - 10$$

Step 3: Simplify:

Calculate the result:

$$12 - 10 = 2$$

Evaluate Expressions

Evaluate the expression when: x = 2

1) $9x + x =$

2) $(8x + 1) + (6x - 8) =$

3) $4x - 9 =$

4) $7 - x =$

5) $9x + 6x + 4x =$

6) $6 + 9x =$

7) $7 + (9x + 6) =$

8) $x + 4 =$

9) $9x + 9x + 3x =$

10) $10x + 7x + 6x =$

Evaluate Expressions

Evaluate the expression when: x = 6

1) $(3x + 5) + (4x - 2) =$

2) $9x - x =$

3) $6x + 10 - 6x =$

4) $x - 8 =$

5) $3x - 10 + 5x =$

6) $x + 4 + 5x =$

7) $x - 9 =$

8) $8 + (6x + 2) =$

9) $9x + 5 =$

10) $2 + (2x + 2) =$

Evaluate Expressions

Evaluate the expression when: x = 1

1) $x - 5 =$

2) $5 - x =$

3) $(3x + 2) + (x - 3) =$

4) $3 + 4x =$

5) $x - 10 =$

6) $x + 3 =$

7) $x - 10 + 4x =$

8) $7x + 10 - 9x =$

9) $6 + (8x + 7) =$

10) $4x + 6 - x =$

Evaluate Expressions

Evaluate the expression when: $x = 6$

1) $3 + x =$

2) $5x - 6 =$

3) $x + 5 =$

4) $x + 7 + (4x - 8) =$

5) $3 + 9x =$

6) $1(3x - 7) + 7(2 + x) =$

7) $x + 2 + 3x =$

8) $10(2x - 4) + 6(5 + x) =$

9) $2x + 9 =$

10) $1 + x =$

Solving Inequalities

Inequalities are mathematical expressions that compare the relative sizes of two values. They are used to express relationships where one quantity is:

- "$<$" (less than),
- "$>$" (greater than),
- "$<=$" (less than or equal to),
- "$>=$" (greater than or equal to),
- and "$\neq$" (not equal to) another quantity.

For example:

$$y + {-10} \leq {-8}$$

To isolate y, we need to get rid of the constant term –10. Since –10 is being subtracted from y, we can undo this operation by adding 10 to both sides of the inequality:

$$y - 10 + 10 \leq -8 + 10$$

$$y \leq 2$$

To check the solution:

$$2 - 10 \leq -8$$

$$-8 = -8$$

The inequality is true when $y = 2$

Solving Inequalities

1)
$$\frac{z}{-2} < -5$$

2)
$$x - 7 \geq 9$$

3)
$$b + -5 > -1$$

4)
$$6 < 3\,m$$

5)

$$-24 > -16\,k$$

6)

$$\frac{m}{4} < 2$$

7)

$$7 > -9 + k$$

8)

$$8 < -6 - y$$

9) $4b < -6$

10) $-9 \leq \dfrac{y}{4}$

11) $-9 - m \leq -6$

12) $-6 + x \leq 6$

13) $b - -8 \geq -3$

14) $-6 \geq 2x$

15) $3 > 5 + y$

16) $3 \leq \dfrac{y}{5}$

17)

$$\frac{z}{-8} \geq -3$$

18)

$$m - -1 \leq 8$$

19)

$$-4 \geq 2\,y$$

20)

$$-10 \leq 2 + y$$

Anna School Learning

Ratio and Proportion

A proportional relationship between two quantities exists when they have a constant ratio or when one is a multiple of the other. In other words, if we increase one quantity, the other quantity will increase or decrease by the same factor. For example, if we double one quantity, the other quantity will also double.

Let's solve a problem:

$$\frac{\square}{9} = \frac{8}{18}$$

Step 1: Cross Multiply: Cross multiply by multiplying the numerator of one fraction by the denominator of the other, and vice versa:

$$x \times 18 = 9 \times 8$$

Step 2: Solve for the Unknown: Perform the multiplication on both sides of the equation:

$$18x = 72$$

Step 3: Divide Both Sides by the Coefficient of the Unknown: To isolate x, divide both sides of the equation by the coefficient of x, which is 18:

$$\frac{18x}{18} = \frac{72}{18}$$

$$x = 4$$

Step 4: Verify Check your solution by substituting x = 4 back into the original equation:

$$\frac{4}{9} = \frac{8}{18}$$

Since both sides are equal, the solution x = 4 is correct.

Ratio and Proportion Word Problems

We can use the concept of proportionality in solving many word problems, for example:

If a car travels 620 miles in six hours, how far can it travel in 12 hours?

Since the car travels a certain distance in a certain amount of time, we can assume that the distance traveled is directly proportional to the time taken.

Let d be the distance the car can travel in 12 hours.

We can set up a proportion:

$$\frac{\text{Distance1}}{\text{Time1}} = \frac{\text{Distance2}}{\text{Time2}}$$

Substituting the given values:

$$\frac{620 \text{ miles}}{6 \text{ hours}} = \frac{d}{12 \text{ hours}}$$

Now, let's solve for d:

$$d = \frac{620 \times 12}{6} = \frac{7440}{6} = 1240$$

So, the car can travel 1240 miles in 12 hours.

Math Workbook for Grade 6-7

Date: ____/____/_____

Proportional Relationship

Solve each Ratio and Proportion.

1) $\frac{8}{\_} = \frac{24}{27}$

2) $\frac{2}{\_} = \frac{20}{30}$

3) $\frac{2}{4} = \frac{\_}{24}$

4) $\frac{2}{\_} = \frac{8}{20}$

5) $\frac{4}{\_} = \frac{16}{36}$

6) $\frac{2}{8} = \frac{16}{\_}$

7) $\frac{1}{\_} = \frac{8}{16}$

8) $\frac{2}{\_} = \frac{16}{48}$

9) $\frac{2}{\_} = \frac{16}{88}$

10) $\frac{4}{10} = \frac{\_}{50}$

11) $\frac{11}{12} = \frac{88}{\_}$

12) $\frac{5}{7} = \frac{45}{\_}$

Anna School Learning

13) $\dfrac{1}{} = \dfrac{10}{90}$

14) $\dfrac{}{4} = \dfrac{21}{28}$

15) $\dfrac{5}{} = \dfrac{35}{42}$

16) $\dfrac{2}{11} = \dfrac{18}{}$

17) $\dfrac{3}{7} = \dfrac{15}{}$

18) $\dfrac{2}{} = \dfrac{6}{15}$

19) $\dfrac{6}{} = \dfrac{30}{40}$

20) $\dfrac{9}{10} = \dfrac{}{60}$

21) $\dfrac{9}{12} = \dfrac{}{36}$

22) $\dfrac{1}{} = \dfrac{4}{12}$

23) $\dfrac{1}{} = \dfrac{2}{4}$

24) $\dfrac{8}{11} = \dfrac{80}{}$

25) $\dfrac{}{5} = \dfrac{24}{40}$

26) $\dfrac{}{10} = \dfrac{35}{70}$

Ratio and Proportion Word Problems

1) If a recipe calls for five cups of sugar for every five cups of flour, how many cups of sugar are needed for 22 cups of flour?

2) If two chefs can bake 100 cakes in 12 hours, how many chefs are needed to bake the same number of cakes in four hours?

3) A car travels 158 miles in three hours. How far can it travel in seven hours?

4) If a recipe calls for three cups of water for every four cups of rice, how much water is needed for seven cups of rice?

5) If a recipe calls for two teaspoon of salt for every five cups of flour, how much salt is needed for 11 cups of flour?

6) A school has a teacher-student ratio of 1:35. If there are 815 students, how many teachers are needed?

7) If 10 workers can build a house in 11 hours, how many workers are needed to build the house in seven hours?

8) If a map scale is 1 inch to three miles, how far apart are two cities that are six inches apart on the map?

9) A school has a ratio of four female teachers to every nine male teachers. If there are 20 male teachers, how many female teachers are there?

10) A machine can produce 109 units of a product in nine hours. How long will it take to produce 333 units?

11) A zoo has a ratio of four monkeys to every seven lions. If there are 48 lions in the zoo, how many monkeys are there?

12) If a square has an area of 130 square meters, what is the length of each side of the square?

13) A train travels 295 miles in five hours. How far can it travel in 11 hours?

14) In a classroom, the ratio of boys to girls is four:nine. If there are 15 girls, how many boys are there?

15) A room has an area of 184 square meters and a length of 14 meters. What is the width of the room?

16) A bike travels at a speed of 17 miles per hour. How long will it take to travel 77 miles?

17) A charity received a donation of $4,967 from a company. If the donation was divided among five charities in the ratio 2:3:4:5:6, how much did the fourth charity receive?

18) A charity received a donation of $3,456 from a company. If the donation was divided among five charities in the ratio 2:3:4:5:6, how much did the fifth charity receive?

19) A recipe calls for five cups of sugar for every eight cups of flour. If you have 12 cups of flour, how much sugar is needed?

20) If seven workers can build a wall in 14 hours, how many workers are needed to build the wall in seven hours?

21) If nine workers can complete a job in 20 days, how many workers are needed to complete the job in six days?

22) A company has a ratio of three managers for every 23 employees. If the company has 105 employees, how many managers are there?

23) If it takes two students 11 hours to complete a science project, how many students are needed to finish the project in six hours?

24) If a recipe calls for six eggs for every eight cups of flour, how many eggs are needed for 20 cups of flour?

25) Savannah sells five desks for every seven Lemons. If there are 57 desks, how many Lemons are there?

26) In a bag of candies, the ratio of chocolate candies to fruit candies is three:six. If there are 14 fruit candies, how many chocolate candies are there?

27) If a team of two construction workers can build a road in 15 days, how many workers are required to complete the road in four days?

28) A road is 148 miles long and it takes a car two hour to travel the entire length. What is the speed of the car in miles per hour?

29) A farmer has a ratio of three sheep to every eight cows in his pasture. If there are 46 cows in the pasture, how many sheep are there?

30) A company has a ratio of two female employees to every eight male employees. If there are 22 male employees, how many female employees are there?

Percentage

Percentage is a way of expressing a number as a fraction of 100. It is commonly used to represent proportions, rates, and comparisons. The symbol "%" is used to denote percentages.

To calculate a percentage, we multiply the given number by the appropriate fraction or decimal equivalent.

How to calculate a percentage:

Convert Percentage to Decimal: If the percentage is given as a percentage value (e.g., 25%), convert it to its decimal equivalent by dividing by 100.

For example, 25% as a decimal is $\frac{25}{100}$ = 0.25

Multiply: Multiply the decimal equivalent of the percentage by the given number. This gives us the portion of the number that represents the percentage.

100 x 0.25 = 25%

Result: The result is the calculated percentage value.

For example, to calculate 25% of 80:

Convert 25% to a decimal: 25% = 0.25.

Multiply 0.25 by 80: 0.25 × 80 = 20. The result is 20.

Percent Word Problems

Percent word problems involve situations where percentages are used to calculate quantities or amounts. These problems often require converting percentages to decimals and then applying them to the given values.

For example:

Bella bought a pair of shoes for $90.00. If she paid an additional 90% for taxes, how much in total did she pay for the shoes?

- Bella bought a pair of shoes for $90.00.
- She paid an additional 90% for taxes.

Calculate 90% of $90:

Tax= 90% × 90

Tax= 0.90 × 90

Tax= $81

Add the tax amount to the original price:

Total cost= $90 + $81

Total cost= $171

Percentage

Find the percentage of given numbers and percent values.

1) 20% of 400 = ☐

2) 15% of ☐ = 45

3) 8% of ☐ = 48

4) 1% of 100 = ☐

5) 5% of 100 = ☐

6) 75% of 800 = ☐

7) ☐ of 200 = 6

8) 6% of ☐ = 54

9) 90% of 700 = ☐

10) 200% of ☐ = 1400

11) 30% of 80 = ☐

12) ☐ of 300 = 30

13) 2% of 700 = ☐

14) 100% of 900 = ☐

15) 4% of 400 = ☐

16) 35% of ☐ = 315

17) 50% of 500 = ☐

18) ☐ of 700 = 560

19) 40% of ☐ = 80

20) 60% of 600 = ☐

21) 70% of ☐ = 49

22) 9% of ☐ = 0.27

23) 7% of 700 = ☐

24) 1% of 800 = ☐

25) ☐ of 300 = 24

26) 80% of 600 = ☐

27) 25% of ☐ = 2

28) 100% of 600 = ☐

Convert Percent and Decimals

1) 60 % = _____

2) 72 % = _____

3) 9 % = _____

4) 90 % = _____

5) 0.06 = _____

6) 42 % = _____

7) 0.87 = _____

8) 0.25 = _____

9) 89 % = _____

10) 0.88 = _____

11) 0.22 = _____

12) 0.16 = _____

13) 45 % = _____

14) 86 % = _____

15) 0.36 = _____

16) 0.66 = _____

17) 0.56 = _____

18) 50 % = _____

19) 43 % = _____

20) 0.64 = _____

21) 0.39 = _____

22) 0.96 = _____

23) 70 % = _____

24) 0.47 = _____

25) 34 % = _____

26) 0.84 = _____

27) 33 % = _____

28) 0.81 = _____

Convert: Ratio, Fraction, Percent, and Decimals

1)

	Ratio	Fraction	Percent	Decimal
a.		3/5		
b.		9/15		
c.		5/11		
d.	1:3			
e.	6:6			
f.	2:3			
g.			25%	
h.		2/4		
i.			29.4%	
j.				0.833
k.			33.3%	
l.		8/14		
m.				0.5
n.		14/19		
o.			50%	

2)

	Ratio	Fraction	Percent	Decimal
a.	8:11			
b.				0.167
c.		11/12		
d.			88.2%	
e.		4/6		
f.				0.789
g.			60%	
h.	2:7			
i.	5:13			
j.		5/10		
k.	7:7			
l.	3:7			
m.				0.625
n.				0.75
o.				0.583

3)

	Ratio	Fraction	Percent	Decimal
a.				1
b.				0.5
c.	7:14			
d.				0.737
e.	11:15			
f.				0.316
g.			63.6%	
h.				0.75
i.		10/15		
j.				0.375
k.				0.182
l.				0.8
m.			5%	
n.			10%	
o.				0.882

Area and Perimeter

The area of a shape represents the amount of space it occupies. The perimeter of a shape is the total distance around its outer edge.

Area of Rectangle

For a square, since all four sides are equal, we only need to know the length of one side to find its area. We can calculate the area of a square by multiplying the length of one side by itself (squared). So, if the length of one side of the square is 's', then the area (A) is given by:

A = s x s

4 in

4 in

A = 4 x 4

A = 16

Perimeter of Rectangle

For a square, since all four sides are equal, we can find the perimeter by adding up the lengths of all four sides. If 's' represents the length of one side, then the perimeter (P) is given by:

$$P = 4 \times s$$

$$P = 4 \times 4$$

$$P = 16$$

Area of Triangle:

The area of a triangle represents the amount of space enclosed within its three sides. The formula for calculating the area of a triangle depends on the type of triangle. For a general triangle, we use the formula:

$$A = \frac{1}{2} \times \text{base} \times \text{height}$$

Where:

- *A* represents the area of the triangle.

- The base is the length of any one side of the triangle.

- The height is the perpendicular distance from the base to the opposite vertex.

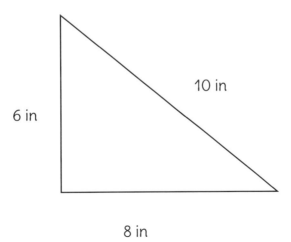

$$A = \frac{1}{2} \times \text{base} \times \text{height}$$

$$A = \frac{1}{2} \times 6 \times 8$$

$$A = \frac{1}{2} \times 48$$

$$A = 24$$

Perimeter of Triangle:

The perimeter of a triangle is the total length of its three sides. To find the perimeter, we simply add the lengths of all three sides together:

$$P = side1 + side2 + side3$$

$$P = 6 + 8 + 10$$

$$P = 24$$

Equilateral Triangle

An equilateral triangle is a triangle in which all three sides are equal in length. To find the area and perimeter of an equilateral triangle, we can use the following formulas:

- Area (A): $\frac{\sqrt{3}}{4} \times a^2$ where a is the length of one side of the equilateral triangle.
- Perimeter (P): $P = 3a$ where a is the length of one side of the equilateral triangle.

Let's solve a problem:

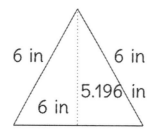

Area of Equilateral Triangle:

$$\text{Area (A): } \frac{\sqrt{3}}{4} \times (6)^2$$

$$\text{Area (A): } \frac{\sqrt{3}}{4} \times 36$$

$$\text{Area (A): } \frac{36\sqrt{3}}{4}$$

$$\text{Area (A): } \frac{36(1.73)}{4}$$

$$\text{Area (A): } \frac{62.35}{4}$$

$$\text{Area (A): } 15.59 \text{ in}^2$$

Perimeter of Equilateral Triangle:

$$P = 3a$$

$$P = 3(6) = 18$$

Isosceles Triangle

An isosceles triangle is a triangle with at least two sides of equal length. The angles opposite the equal sides are also equal.

Area of Isosceles Triangle

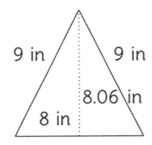

$$A = \frac{1}{2} \times \text{base} \times \text{height}$$

$$A = \frac{1}{2} \times 8 \times 8$$

$$A = \frac{1}{2} \times 64$$

$$A = 32$$

Perimeter of Isosceles Triangle

The perimeter of a triangle is the total length of its three sides. To find the perimeter, we simply add the lengths of all three sides together:

$$P = side1 + side2 + side3$$

$$P = 9 + 9 + 8$$

$$P = 26$$

Scalene Triangle

A scalene triangle is a triangle with no equal sides and no equal angles. The formula for finding various properties of a scalene triangle is as follows:

Area (A): The area of a scalene triangle can be calculated using Heron's fo rmula, which is given by:

$$A = \sqrt{s(s-a)(s-b)(s-c)}$$

where s is the semi-perimeter of the triangle,

and a, b, and c are the lengths of its three sides.

Perimeter (P): The perimeter of a scalene triangle is the sum of the lengths of its three sides.

$$P = side1 + side2 + side3$$

Let's find the Area and Perimeter of a Scalene Triangle:

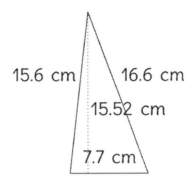

Area (A): First, we calculate the semi-perimeter (*s*):

$$S = \frac{a+b+c}{2} = \frac{15.6 + 16.6 + 7.7}{2} = \frac{39.8}{2} = 19.9 \text{ cm}$$

Heron's formula to find the area:

$$A = \sqrt{s(s-a)(s-b)(s-c)}$$

$$A = \sqrt{19.9(19.9-15.6)(19.9-16.6)(19.9-7.7)}$$

$$A = \sqrt{19.9 \times 4.3 \times 3.3 \times 12.2}$$

$$A = \sqrt{3445} \approx 59$$

Perimeter (P):

$$P = side1 + side2 + side3$$

$$P = 15.6 + 16.6 + 7.7$$

$$P = 39.8$$

Anna School Learning

Area and Perimeter of an L-shape

The L-shaped figure typically consists of two rectangles joined together to form an L-shape. To find the area and perimeter of an L-shaped figure, we will need to calculate the areas and perimeters of each rectangle and then combine them.

Area=Area of Rectangle 1 + Area of Rectangle 2

Perimeter=Perimeter of Rectangle 1 + Perimeter of Rectangle 2

Let's find the Area and Perimeter of an L-shape:

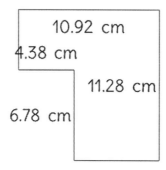

10.92 cm

4.38 cm

11.28 cm

6.78 cm

Area of L-Shape

Area 1 = 4.38 x 4.5 = 19.7 cm^2

Area 2 = 11.28 x 6.54 = 73.7 cm^2

Area = 19.7 + 73.7

Area = 93.481 cm^2

Perimeter of L-Shape

P = 11.28 + 6.54 + 6.78 + 4.38 + 4.5 + 10.92

P = 44.4 cm

Area and Perimeter of U-shape

U-shape is basically composed of three rectangles, we'll need to calculate the area and perimeter of each rectangle separately and then sum them up.

Area of the U-shape:

The total area (A) of the U-shape is the sum of the areas of the three rectangles:

$$A = A1 + A2 + A3$$

Perimeter of the U-shape: The total perimeter (P) of the U-shape is the sum of the perimeters of the three rectangles:

$$P = P1 + P2 + P3$$

Let's find the area and perimeter of the following U-shape:

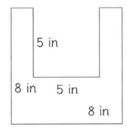

Area:

$$A1 = 8 \times 1.5 = 12 + A2 = 3 \times 5 = 15 + A3 = 8 \times 1.5 = 12$$

$$= 12 + 15 + 12$$

$$= 39 \text{ in}^2$$

Perimeter:

$$2 \times 8 + 2 \times 5 + 2 \times 8$$

$$= 16 + 10 + 16$$

$$= 42$$

Area and Perimeter

1)

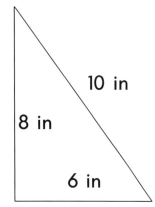

10 in
8 in
6 in

2)

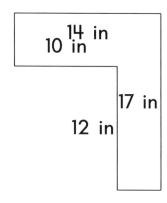

14 in
10 in
17 in
12 in

3)

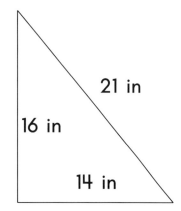

21 in
16 in
14 in

4)

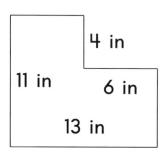

4 in
11 in
6 in
13 in

5)

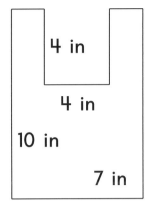

4 in

4 in

10 in

7 in

6)

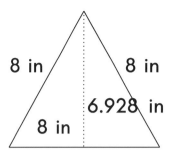

8 in

8 in

6.928 in

8 in

7)

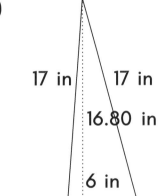

17 in

17 in

16.80 in

6 in

8)

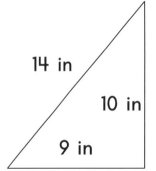

14 in

10 in

9 in

9)

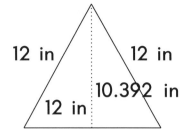

12 in   12 in

10.392 in

12 in

10)

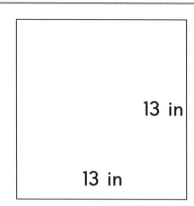

13 in

13 in

11)

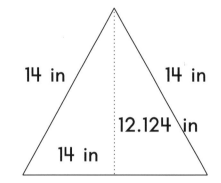

14 in   14 in

12.124 in

14 in

12)

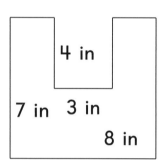

4 in

7 in   3 in

8 in

13)

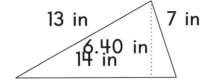

13 in   7 in
6.40 in
14 in

14)

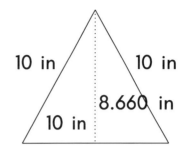

10 in   10 in
8.660 in
10 in

15)

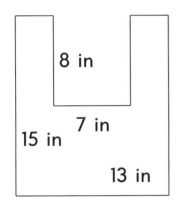

8 in
7 in
15 in
13 in

16)

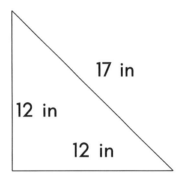

17 in
12 in
12 in

17)

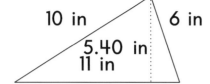

10 in   6 in
5.40 in
11 in

18)

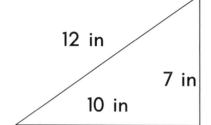

12 in
7 in
10 in

19)

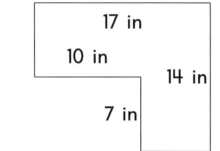

17 in
10 in
14 in
7 in

20)

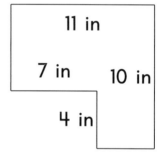

11 in
7 in   10 in
4 in

21)

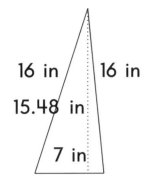

16 in

16 in

15.48 in

7 in

22)

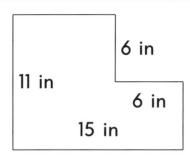

6 in

11 in

6 in

15 in

23)

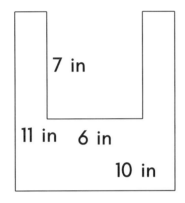

7 in

11 in   6 in

10 in

24)

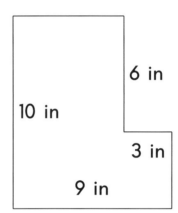

6 in

10 in

3 in

9 in

25)

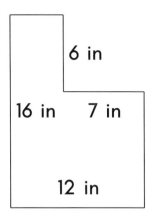

6 in

16 in   7 in

12 in

26)

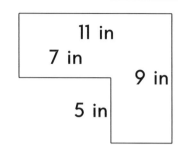

11 in

7 in

9 in

5 in

27)

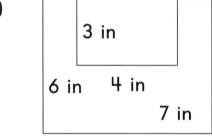

3 in

6 in   4 in

7 in

28)

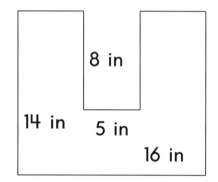

8 in

14 in   5 in

16 in

29)

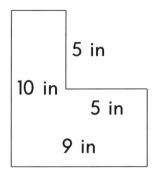

5 in

10 in

5 in

9 in

30)

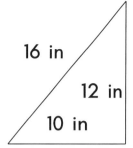

16 in

12 in

10 in

31)

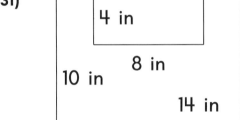

4 in

8 in

10 in

14 in

32)

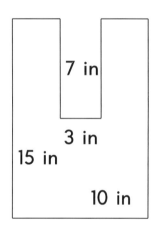

7 in

3 in

15 in

10 in

33)

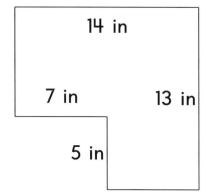

14 in

7 in   13 in

5 in

34)

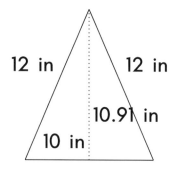

12 in   12 in

10.91 in

10 in

35)

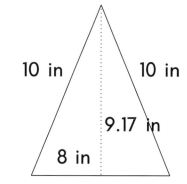

10 in   10 in

9.17 in

8 in

36)

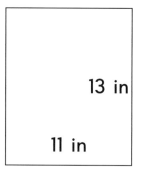

13 in

11 in

37)

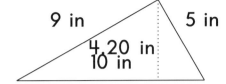

9 in   5 in   4.20 in   10 in

38)

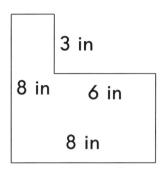

3 in   8 in   6 in   8 in

39)

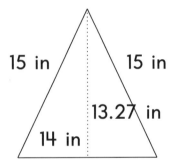

15 in   15 in   13.27 in   14 in

40)

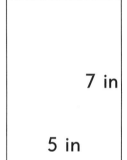

7 in   5 in

Area and Circumference of circles

To find the area (A) and circumference (C) of a circle, we use the following formulas:

1. **Area of a Circle (A) = $\pi \times (radius)^2$**
   - where π (pi) is a constant with value of (3.14). It is a ratio of the circumference of a circle to its diameter,
   - the radius (r) is the distance from the center of the circle.
2. **Circumference of a Circle (C) = $2 \times \pi \times radius$**

Let's solve an example: suppose a swimming pool has a radius of 11 meters, we are required to calculate its Area and Circumference:

$$\text{Area } (A) = \pi \times (radius)^2$$

$$A = 3.14 \times 11^2$$

$$A = 3.14 \times 121$$

$$A = 379.94 \text{ square meters}$$

$$\text{Circumference } (C) = 2 \times \pi \times radius$$

$$C = 2 \times 3.14 \times 11$$

$$C = 69.08 \text{ square meters}$$

Circumference and Area of circles

Calculate the circumference of each circle. Pi Value = 3.14

1)

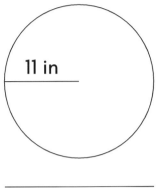

11 in

_____

_____

2)

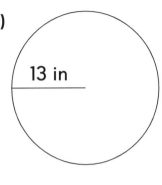

13 in

_____

_____

3)

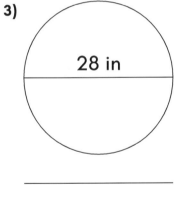

28 in

_____

_____

4)

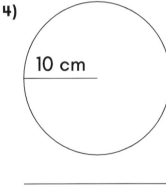

10 cm

_____

_____

5)

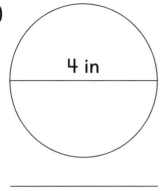

4 in

_____

_____

6)

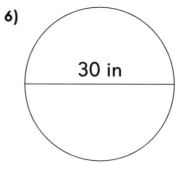

30 in

_____

_____

7)

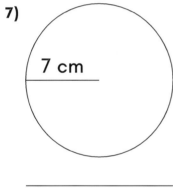

7 cm

_____

_____

8)

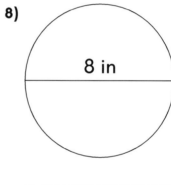

8 in

_____

_____

9)

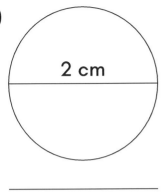

2 cm

_____

_____

10)

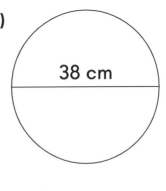

38 cm

_____

_____

11)

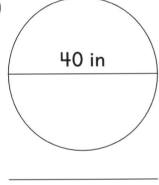

40 in

_____

_____

12)

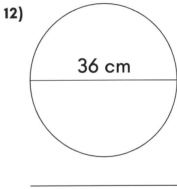

36 cm

_____

_____

13)

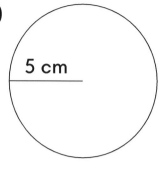

5 cm

_____

_____

14)

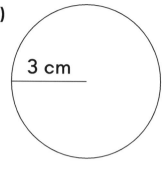

3 cm

_____

_____

15)

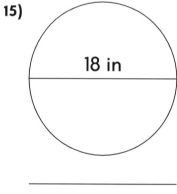

18 in

_____

_____

16)

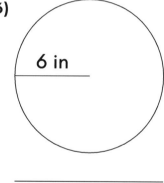

6 in

_____

_____

17)

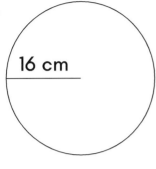

16 cm

_____

_____

18)

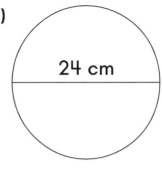

24 cm

_____

_____

19)

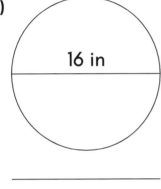

16 in

_____

_____

20)

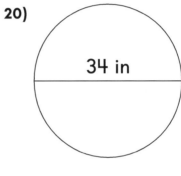

34 in

_____

_____

Angles

Types of Angles: Angles can be classified based on their measures:

- **Acute Angle:** An angle less than 90°.

- **Right Angle:** An angle exactly equal to 90°.

- **Obtuse Angle:** An angle greater than 90° and less than 180°.

- **Straight Angle:** An angle exactly equal to 180°.

- **Reflex Angle:** An angle greater than 180° and less than 360°.

- **Full Angle:** An angle equal to 360°.

Measure angles with a protractor. It looks like a semicircle or a half-disc with degree markings from 0° to 180°. To measure an angle using a protractor, we place the center of the protractor at the vertex of the angle, align one side of the angle with the zero mark on the protractor, and read the degree measure where the other side intersects the protractor.

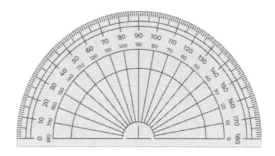

For example, let's measure the following angle.

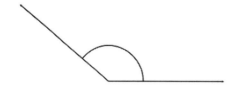

The angle is 140°.

We also know that the angle is greater than 90° and less than 180°, so this is an Obtuse angle.

Classify and Measure Angles

1)

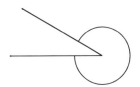

_____

2)

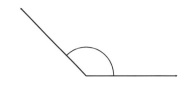

_____

3)

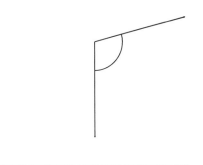

_____

4)

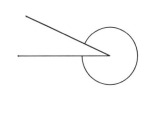

_____

5)

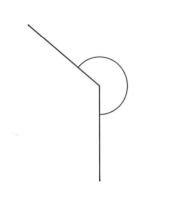

_____

6)

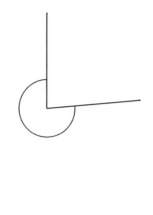

_____

7)

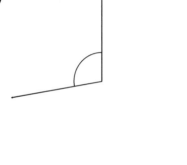

_____

8)

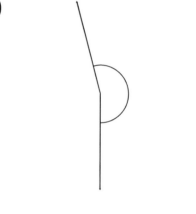

_____

9)

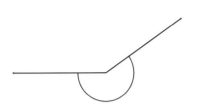

_____

10)

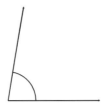

_____

11)

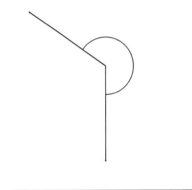

_____

12)

_____

13)

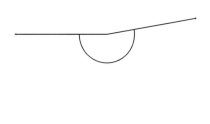

_____

14)

_____

15)

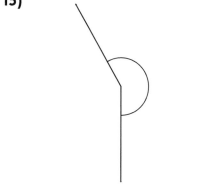

_____

16)

_____

17)

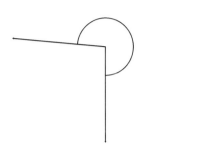

18)

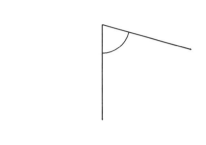

19)

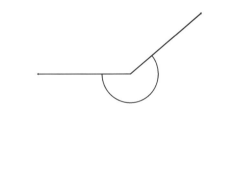

20)

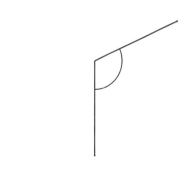

21)

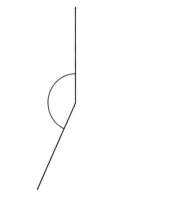

22)

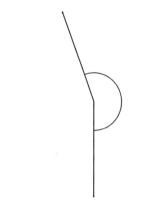

23)

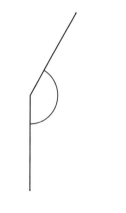

24)

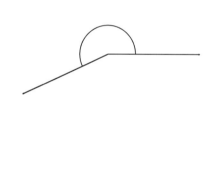

25)

_____

26)

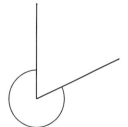

_____

27)

_____

28)

_____

Volume and surface Area

Volume refers to the amount of space occupied by a three-dimensional object. For shapes like cubes or rectangular prisms, we calculate volume by multiplying their length, width, and height.

To find the volume *V* of a rectangular prism, we use the formula:

$$Volume = length\ x\ width\ x\ height$$

Surface Area represents the total area covering all the faces of a three-dimensional object. For shapes like cubes or rectangular prisms, we find the surface area by summing the areas of all its faces.

The formula for surface area *SA* of a cube or rectangular prism is:

$$Surface\ Area = 2lw + 2lh + 2wh$$

Where: l is the length, w is the width, and h is the height of the object.

For example: Let's find the Volume and Surface Area of following rectangular prisms:

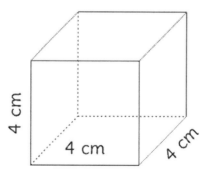

$$Volume = length \times width \times height$$

$$= 4 \times 4 \times 4$$

$$= 64\ cm^2$$

$$Surface\ Area = 2lw + 2lh + 2wh$$

$$= 2(4 \times 4) + 2(4 \times 4) + 2(4 \times 4)$$

$$= 32 + 32 + 32$$

$$= 96 \text{ cm2}$$

Different 3D objects have unique formulas for finding their volume and surface area. Here are some common ones:

1. **Cube:**

   - Volume: $V = s^3$ (where s is the length of one side of the cube)

   - Surface area: $SA = 6s^2$

2. **Sphere:**

   - Volume: $V = (\frac{4}{3})\pi r^3$ (where r is the radius of the sphere)

   - Surface area: $SA = 4\pi r^2$

3. **Cone:**

   - Volume: $V = (\frac{1}{3})\pi r^2 h$ (where r is the radius of the base and h is the height of the cone)

   - Surface area: $SA = \pi r^2 + \pi r\sqrt{(r^2 + h^2)}$

4. **Cylinder:**

   - Volume: $V = \pi r^2 h$ (where r is the radius of the base and h is the height of the cylinder)

   - Surface area: $SA = 2\pi r^2 + 2\pi rh$

5. **Pyramid:**

   - Volume: $V = (\frac{1}{3})Bh$ (where B is the area of the base and h is the height of the pyramid)

   - Surface area: $SA = B + \frac{1}{2}Pl$ (where P is the perimeter of the base and l is the slant height of the pyramid)

Volume and Surface Area

1)

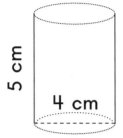

2)

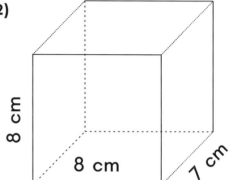

3)

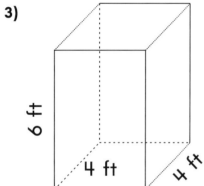

4)

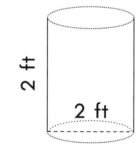

5)

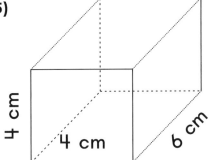

4 cm

4 cm

6 cm

6)

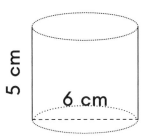

5 cm

6 cm

7)

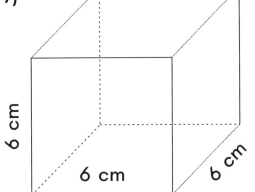

6 cm

6 cm

6 cm

8)

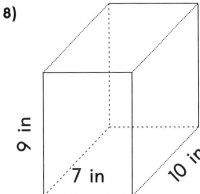

9 in

7 in

10 in

9)

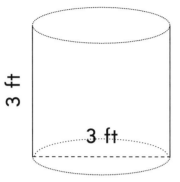

3 ft

3 ft

10)

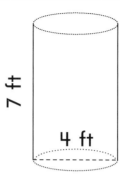

7 ft

4 ft

11)

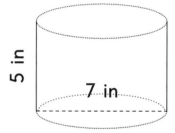

5 in

7 in

12)

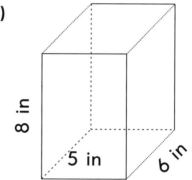

8 in

5 in

6 in

13)

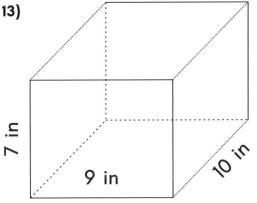

14)

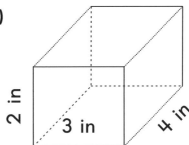

15)

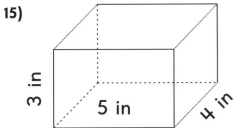

16)

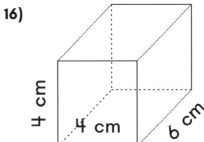

17)

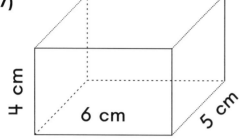

18)

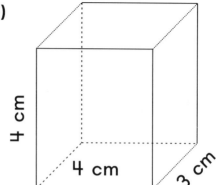

19)

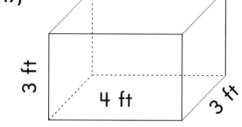

20)

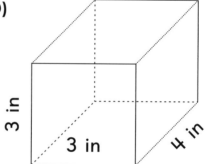

21)

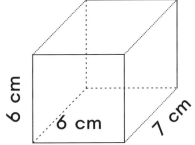

6 cm

6 cm

7 cm

22)

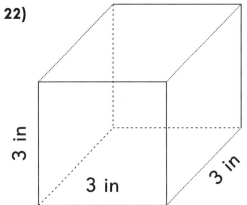

3 in

3 in

3 in

23)

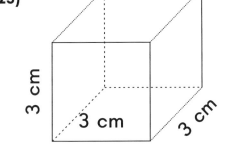

3 cm

3 cm

3 cm

24)

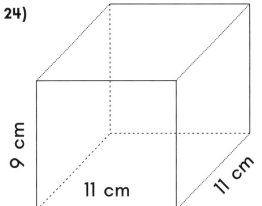

9 cm

11 cm

11 cm

25)

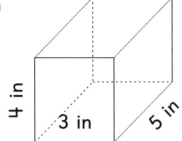

26)

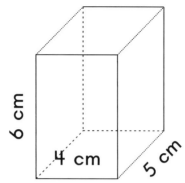

27)

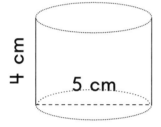

28)

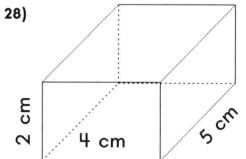

Statistics

Mean

The mean, also known as the average, is a measure of central tendency.
To find the mean of a set of numbers:
- Add up all the numbers in the set.
- Divide the sum by the total count of numbers in the set.

For example: consider the set of numbers: 70, 72, 49, 69, 27, 76.

$$\text{Mean} = \frac{70 + 72 + 49 + 69 + 27 + 76}{6}$$

$$= \frac{363}{6} = 60.5$$

Median

The median is a measure of central tendency that represents the middle value of a dataset when the values are arranged in ascending or descending order.
To find the median of a set of numbers:
- Arrange the numbers in ascending or descending order.
- If the total count of numbers is odd, the median is the middle value.
- If the total count of numbers is even, the median is the average of the two middle values.

For example: consider the set of numbers: 70, 72, 49, 69, 27, 76.

$$27, 49, 69, 70, 72, 76$$

$$\text{Median} = \frac{69 + 70}{2} = \frac{139}{2} = 69.5$$

Mode:

The mode in statistics refers to the value that appears most frequently in a given set of data.

Let's consider the following set of numbers:

$$\{2, 4, 4, 5, 6, 6, 6, 7, 8, 8\}$$

In this set, the number 6 appears three times, more than any other number. Therefore, the mode of this dataset is 6.

It's possible for a dataset to have more than one mode if two or more numbers appear with the same highest frequency. In such cases, the dataset is considered multimodal. If no number repeats, the dataset is considered to have no mode.

For example:

$$\{2, 4, 4, 4, 5, 6, 6, 6, 7, 8, 8\}$$

In this date set, 4 and 6 appear three times. Therefore, this dataset is multimodal.

Range:

In statistics, the range refers to the difference between the largest and smallest values in a dataset. It represents the spread or variability of the data.

For example, consider the dataset { 68, 13, 30, 18, 45, 76, 11}:

To calculate the range:

1. Arrange the data points in ascending order.

$$11, 13, 18, 30, 45, 68, 76$$

2. Subtract the smallest value from the largest value.

- The smallest value is 11.
- The largest value is 76.

Range = Largest value - smallest value = 76 - 11 = 65.

Mean, Median, Mode, and Range

Find the Mean, Median, Mode and Range of the following sets of data.

1) 62, 24, 93, 62, 90, 5

   Mean = _____   Median = _____

   Mode = _____   Range = _____

2) 2, 98, 45, 92, 75, 43

   Mean = _____   Median = _____

   Mode = _____   Range = _____

3) 2, 75, 9, 49, 40, 21

   Mean = _____   Median = _____

   Mode = _____   Range = _____

4) 50, 12, 60, 60, 6, 5

   Mean = _____   Median = _____

   Mode = _____   Range = _____

5) 33, 27, 13, 7, 14, 61, 68

Mean = _____ Median = ____

Mode = _____ Range = ____

6) 29, 9, 9, 66, 47, 58, 51

Mean = _____ Median = ____

Mode = _____ Range = ____

7) 14, 35, 84, 12, 74, 29

Mean = _____ Median = ____

Mode = _____ Range = ____

8) 27, 7, 7, 93, 31, 78

Mean = ____ Median = ____

Mode = ____ Range = ____

9) 50, 89, 96, 67, 68, 2

Mean = ____ Median = ____

Mode = ____ Range = ____

10) 19, 88, 29, 63, 91, 94

Mean = _____   Median = _____

Mode = _____   Range = _____

11) 85, 84, 24, 46, 34, 93, 9

Mean = _____   Median = _____

Mode = _____   Range = _____

12) 61, 91, 89, 8, 16, 28, 48

Mean = _____   Median = _____

Mode = _____   Range = _____

13) 86, 76, 78, 26, 21, 19

Mean = _____   Median = _____

Mode = _____   Range = _____

14) 75, 35, 11, 79, 33, 42

Mean = _____   Median = _____

Mode = _____   Range = _____

15) 40, 64, 29, 70, 22, 51, 43

Mean = _____ Median = _____

Mode = _____ Range = _____

16) 89, 27, 90, 5, 80, 73

Mean = _____ Median = _____

Mode = _____ Range = _____

17) 13, 84, 70, 87, 61, 82

Mean = _____ Median = _____

Mode = _____ Range = _____

18) 80, 39, 21, 16, 42, 10, 4

Mean = _____ Median = _____

Mode = _____ Range = _____

19) 42, 72, 19, 50, 73, 44, 14

Mean = _____ Median = _____

Mode = _____ Range = _____

20) 91, 54, 45, 33, 22, 68, 56

Mean = _____   Median = _____

Mode = _____   Range = _____

21) 73, 39, 21, 95, 71, 98, 52

Mean = _____   Median = _____

Mode = _____   Range = _____

22) 8, 35, 6, 48, 50, 97

Mean = _____   Median = _____

Mode = _____   Range = _____

23) 52, 3, 19, 48, 87, 60, 18

Mean = _____   Median = _____

Mode = _____   Range = _____

24) 9, 70, 70, 76, 17, 61

Mean = _____   Median = _____

Mode = _____   Range = _____

ANSWERS

Page 1: Positive and Negative Integers

1. 11   **2.** –5   **3.** –26   **4.** –19   **5.** –10   **6.** –3   **7.** –7   **8.** –23   **9.** –22

10. 9   **11.** –3   **12.** 5   **13.** 7   **14.** –10   **15.** –18   **16.** 11   **17.** –12   **18.** 6

19. –19   **20.** 3   **21.** –1   **22.** 2   **23.** 0   **24.** 16   **25.** 2   **26.** 4   **27.** 13

28. 9   **29.** –10   **30.** –18

Page 7: Exponents

1. 1/2197   **2.** 1/512   **3.** 1,000   **4.** 625   **5.** 361   **6.** 1/324

7. 1/2744   **8.** 6,561   **9.** 14,641   **10.** 216   **11.** 121   **12.** 343

13. 38,416   **14.** 1   **15.** 1   **16.** 1/9   **17.** 2,401   **18.** 160,000

19. 1/1000   **20.** 1/36   **21.** 1/81   **22.** 104,976   **23.** 1,331   **24.** 4,096

Page 9: Square and Cube Roots

1. 5   **2.** 4   **3.** 21   **4.** 3   **5.** 3   **6.** 2   **7.** 9   **8.** 99   **9.** 53   **10.** 6

11. 44   **12.** 1   **13.** 15   **14.** 10   **15.** 5   **16.** 17   **17.** 1   **18.** 4   **19.** 20   **20.** 14

21. 7   **22.** 19   **23.** 10   **24.** 30   **25.** 7   **26.** 81   **27.** 2   **28.** 6   **29.** 31   **30.** 13

Page 11: Factors

1. None   **2.** None   **3.** None

4. 2, 29   **5.** 2, 4, 11, 22   **6.** 2, 4

7. None   **8.** 2, 23   **9.** 2

10. 2, 4, 8, 16   **11.** None   **12.** None

13. 2, 4, 7, 14   **14.** 2, 7, 14, 49   **15.** None

16. 7   **17.** 3, 5   **18.** 3, 23

19. None   **20.** None   **21.** 3

22. 2, 3   **23.** 2, 3, 6, 13, 26, 39   **24.** 3, 5, 15, 25

Page 14: Multiples

1. 20, 40, 60, 80, 100   **2.** 11, 22, 33, 44, 55   **3.** 3, 6, 9, 12, 15

4. 2, 4, 6, 8, 10   **5.** 62, 124, 186, 248, 310   **6.** 17, 34, 51, 68, 85

7. 25, 50, 75, 100, 125   **8.** 6, 12, 18, 24, 30   **9.** 8, 16, 24, 32, 40

10. 9, 18, 27, 36, 45   **11.** 13, 26, 39, 52, 65   **12.** 93, 186, 279, 372, 465

13. 7, 14, 21, 28, 35   **14.** 56, 112, 168, 224, 280   **15.** 74, 148, 222, 296, 370

16. 19, 38, 57, 76, 95   **17.** 39, 78, 117, 156, 195   **18.** 72, 144, 216, 288, 360

19. 27, 54, 81, 108, 135   **20.** 79, 158, 237, 316, 395   **21.** 26, 52, 78, 104, 130

22. 64, 128, 192, 256, 320   **23.** 1, 2, 3, 4, 5   **24.** 44, 88, 132, 176, 220

Page 17:   Order of Operations (PEMDAS)

1. 15   **2.** 5   **3.** 289   **4.** 2.4   **5.** 11   **6.** 26   **7.** 100

8. 14   **9.** 20   **10.** 50   **11.** 24   **12.** 205   **13.** 31   **14.** 3,137

15. 10   **16.** –6   **17.** 36   **18.** 4   **19.** 100   **20.** 13   **21.** 19

22. 2,405   **23.** 46   **24.** 19   **25.** –1   **26.** 40   **27.** 1.6   **28.** 17

29. 13   **30.** 1.3

Page 20:   Solving Equations: (One Side)

1. $x = 15$ **2.** $x = 18$ **3.** $x = 10$ **4.** $x = 2$ **5.** $x = 11$ **6.** $x = 7$ **7.** $x = 6$

8. $x = 1$ **9.** $x = 18$ **10.** $x = 3$ **11.** $x = 14$ **12.** $x = 12$ **13.** $x = 19$ **14.** $x = 8$

15. $x = 18$ **16.** $x = 5$ **17.** $x = 6$ **18.** $x = 14$ **19.** $x = 7$ **20.** $x = 36$ **21.** $x = 16$

22. $x = 18$ **23.** $x = 2$ **24.** $x = 16$ **25.** $x = 18$ **26.** $x = 14$ **27.** $x = 20$ **28.** $x = 13$

29. $x = 27$ **30.** $x = 13$

Page 23:   Evaluate Expressions

1. 20   **2.** 21   **3.** –1   **4.** 5   **5.** 38   **6.** 24   **7.** 31   **8.** 6   **9.** 42   **10.** 46

Page 24:   Evaluate Expressions

1. 45   **2.** 48   **3.** 10   **4.** –2   **5.** 38   **6.** 40   **7.** –3   **8.** 46   **9.** 59   **10.** 16

Page 25:   Evaluate Expressions

1. –4   **2.** 4   **3.** 3   **4.** 7   **5.** –9   **6.** 4   **7.** –5   **8.** 8   **9.** 21   **10.** 9

Page 26:   Evaluate Expressions

1. 9   **2.** 24   **3.** 11   **4.** 29   **5.** 57   **6.** 67   **7.** 26   **8.** 146   **9.** 21   **10.** 7

Page 27:   Solving Inequalities

1. $z > 10$ **2.** $x \geq 16$ **3.** $b > 4$ **4.** $m > 2$ **5.** $k > 3/2$ **6.** $m < 8$

7. $k < 16$ **8.** $y < -14$ **9.** $b < -3/2$ **10.** $y \geq -36$ **11.** $m \geq -3$ **12.** $x \leq 12$

13. $b \geq -11$ **14.** $x \leq -3$ **15.** $y < -2$ **16.** $y \geq 15$ **17.** $z \leq 24$ **18.** $m \leq 7$

19. $y \le -2$ **20.** $y \ge -12$

Page 32: Proportional Relationship

1. 9	**2.** 3	**3.** 12	**4.** 5	**5.** 9	**6.** 64	**7.** 2	**8.** 6	**9.** 11	**10.** 20

1. 9 **2.** 3 **3.** 12 **4.** 5 **5.** 9 **6.** 64 **7.** 2 **8.** 6 **9.** 11 **10.** 20

11. 96 **12.** 63 **13.** 9 **14.** 3 **15.** 6 **16.** 99 **17.** 35 **18.** 5 **19.** 8 **20.** 54

21. 27 **22.** 3 **23.** 2 **24.** 110 **25.** 3 **26.** 5

Page 34: Ratio and Proportion Word Problems

1. 22 **2.** 6 **3.** 368.67 **4.** 5.25 **5.** 4.4 **6.** 23.29

7. 15.71 **8.** 18 **9.** 8.89 **10.** 27.50 **11.** 27.43 **12.** 11.40

13. 649 **14.** 6.67 **15.** 13.14 **16.** 4.53 **17.** 1,241.75 **18.** 1,036.8

19. 7.5 **20.** 14 **21.** 30 **22.** 13.70 **23.** 3.67 **24.** 15

25. 79.8 **26.** 7 **27.** 7.5 **28.** 74 **29.** 17.25 **30.** 5.5

Page 44: Percentage

1. 80 **2.** 300 **3.** 600 **4.** 1 **5.** 5 **6.** 600 **7.** 3% **8.** 900

9. 630 **10.** 700 **11.** 24 **12.** 10% **13.** 14 **14.** 900 **15.** 16 **16.** 900

17. 250 **18.** 80% **19.** 200 **20.** 360 **21.** 70 **22.** 3 **23.** 49 **24.** 8

25. 8% **26.** 480 **27.** 8 **28.** 600

Page 46: Convert Percent and Decimals

1. 0.6 **2.** 0.72 **3.** 0.09 **4.** 0.9 **5.** 6% **6.** 0.42 **7.** 87% **8.** 25%

9. 0.89 **10.** 88% **11.** 22% **12.** 16% **13.** 0.45 **14.** 0.86 **15.** 36% **16.** 66%

17. 56% **18.** 0.5 **19.** 0.43 **20.** 64% **21.** 39% **22.** 96% **23.** 0.7 **24.** 47%

25. 0.34 **26.** 84% **27.** 0.33 **28.** 81%

Page 48: Convert: Ratio, Fraction, Percent, and Decimals

1.

	Ratio	Fraction	Percent	Decimal
a.	3:5	3/5	60%	0.6
b.	9:15	9/15	60%	0.6
c.	5:11	5/11	45.5%	0.455
d.	1:3	1/3	33.3%	0.333
e.	6:6	6/6	100%	1
f.	2:3	2/3	66.7%	0.667
g.	4:16	4/16	25%	0.25
h.	2:4	2/4	50%	0.5
i.	5:17	5/17	29.4%	0.294
j.	10:12	10/12	83.3%	0.833
k.	2:6	2/6	33.3%	0.333
l.	8:14	8/14	57.1%	0.571
m.	9:18	9/18	50%	0.5
n.	14:19	14/19	73.7%	0.737
o.	1:2	1/2	50%	0.5

2.

	Ratio	Fraction	Percent	Decimal
a.	8:11	8/11	72.7%	0.727
b.	2:12	2/12	16.7%	0.167
c.	11:12	11/12	91.7%	0.917
d.	15:17	15/17	88.2%	0.882
e.	4:6	4/6	66.7%	0.667
f.	15:19	15/19	78.9%	0.789
g.	6:10	6/10	60%	0.6
h.	2:7	2/7	28.6%	0.286
i.	5:13	5/13	38.5%	0.385
j.	5:10	5/10	50%	0.5
k.	7:7	7/7	100%	1
l.	3:7	3/7	42.9%	0.429
m.	10:16	10/16	62.5%	0.625
n.	6:8	6/8	75%	0.75
o.	7:12	7/12	58.3%	0.583

3.

	Ratio	Fraction	Percent	Decimal
a.	14:14	14/14	100%	1
b.	3:6	3/6	50%	0.5
c.	7:14	7/14	50%	0.5
d.	14:19	14/19	73.7%	0.737
e.	11:15	11/15	73.3%	0.733
f.	6:19	6/19	31.6%	0.316
g.	7:11	7/11	63.6%	0.636
h.	3:4	3/4	75%	0.75
i.	10:15	10/15	66.7%	0.667
j.	3:8	3/8	37.5%	0.375
k.	2:11	2/11	18.2%	0.182
l.	4:5	4/5	80%	0.8
m.	1:20	1/20	5%	0.05
n.	1:10	1/10	10%	0.1
o.	15:17	15/17	88.2%	0.882

Page 51:   Area and Perimeter

1. P=24 A=24	**2.** P=62 A=118	**3.** P=51 A=112	**4.** P=48 A=119
5. P=42 A=54	**6.** P=24 A=27.71	**7.** P=40 A=50.4	**8.** P=33 A=45
9. P=36 A=62.35	**10.** P=52 A=169	**11.** P=42 A=84.87	**12.** P=38 A=44
13. P=34 A=44.8	**14.** P=30 A=43.3	**15.** P=72 A=139	**16.** P=41 A=72
17. P=27 A=29.7	**18.** P=29 A=35	**19.** P=62 A=168	**20.** P=42 A=82
21. P=39 A=54.18	**22.** P=52 A=129	**23.** P=56 A=68	**24.** P=38 A=72
25. P=56 A=150	**26.** P=40 A=64	**27.** P=32 A=30	**28.** P=76 A=184
29. P=38 A=65	**30.** P=38 A=60	**31.** P=56 A=108	**32.** P=64 A=129
33. P=54 A=147	**34.** P=34 A=54.55	**35.** P=28 A=36.68	**36.** P=48 A=143
37. P=24 A=21	**38.** P=32 A=46	**39.** P=44 A=92.89	**40.** P=24 A=35

Page 61:   Circumference and Area of circles

1. C=69.08 in A=379.94 in^2	**2.** C=81.64 in A=530.66 in^2
3. C=87.92 in A=615.44 in^2	**4.** C=62.80 cm A=314.00 cm^2
5. C=12.56 in A=12.56 in^2	**6.** C=94.20 in A=706.50 in^2
7. C=43.96 cm A=153.86 cm^2	**8.** C=25.12 in A=50.24 in^2
9. C=6.28 cm A=3.14 cm^2	**10.** C=119.32 cm A=1,133.54 cm^2
11. C=125.60 in A=1,256.00 in^2	**12.** C=113.04 cm A=1,017.36 cm^2
13. C=31.40 cm A=78.50 cm^2	**14.** C=18.84 cm A=28.26 cm^2
15. C=56.52 in A=254.34 in^2	**16.** C=37.68 in A=113.04 in^2
17. C=100.48 cm A=803.84 cm^2	**18.** C=75.36 cm A=452.16 cm^2
19. C=50.24 in A=200.96 in^2	**20.** C=106.76 in A=907.46 in^2

Page 66:   Classify and Measure Angles

1. 330° Reflex	**2.** 135° Obtuse	**3.** 105° Obtuse	**4.** 335° Reflex
5. 230° Reflex	**6.** 275° Reflex	**7.** 100° Obtuse	**8.** 195° Reflex
9. 215° Reflex	**10.** 80° Acute	**11.** 235° Reflex	**12.** 60° Acute
13. 190° Reflex	**14.** 350° Reflex	**15.** 210° Reflex	**16.** 60° Acute
17. 265° Reflex	**18.** 75° Acute	**19.** 220° Reflex	**20.** 115° Obtuse

21. 155° Obtuse   **22.** 200° Reflex   **23.** 150° Obtuse   **24.** 205° Reflex

25. 50° Acute   **26.** 295° Reflex   **27.** 10° Acute   **28.** 350° Reflex

Page 73: Volume and Surface Area

1. V=62.83 cm³ cm³ SA=88 cm² cm²   **2.** V=448 cm³ cm³ SA=352 cm² cm²

3. V=96 ft³ ft³ SA=128 ft² ft²   **4.** V=6.28 ft³ ft³ SA=19 ft² ft²

5. V=96 cm³ cm³ SA=128 cm² cm²   **6.** V=141.37 cm³ cm³ SA=151 cm² cm²

7. V=216 cm³ cm³ SA=216 cm² cm²   **8.** V=630 in³ in³ SA=446 in² in²

9. V=21.21 ft³ ft³ SA=42 ft² ft²   **10.** V=87.96 ft³ ft³ SA=113 ft² ft²

11. V=192.42 in³ in³ SA=187 in² in²   **12.** V=240 in³ in³ SA=236 in² in²

13. V=630 in³ in³ SA=446 in² in²   **14.** V=24 in³ in³ SA=52 in² in²

15. V=60 in³ in³ SA=94 in² in²   **16.** V=96 cm³ cm³ SA=128 cm² cm²

17. V=120 cm³ cm³ SA=148 cm² cm²   **18.** V=48 cm³ cm³ SA=80 cm² cm²

19. V=36 ft³ ft³ SA=66 ft² ft²   **20.** V=36 in³ in³ SA=66 in² in²

21. V=252 cm³ cm³ SA=240 cm² cm²   **22.** V=27 in³ in³ SA=54 in² in²

23. V=27 cm³ cm³ SA=54 cm² cm²   **24.** V=1,089 cm³ cm³ SA=638 cm² cm²

25. V=60 in³ in³ SA=94 in² in²   **26.** V=120 cm³ cm³ SA=148 cm² cm²

27. V=78.54 cm³ cm³ SA=102 cm² cm²   **28.** V=40 cm³ cm³ SA=76 cm² cm²

Page 80: Mean, Median, Mode, and Range

1. Mean = 56, Median = 62, Mode = 62, Range = 88

2. Mean = 59.167, Median = 60, Mode = none, Range = 96

3. Mean = 32.667, Median = 30.5, Mode = none, Range = 73

4. Mean = 32.167, Median = 31, Mode = 60, Range = 55

5. Mean = 31.857, Median = 27, Mode = none, Range = 61

6. Mean = 38.429, Median = 47, Mode = 9, Range = 57

7. Mean = 41.333, Median = 32, Mode = none, Range = 72

8. Mean = 40.5, Median = 29, Mode = 7, Range = 86

9. Mean = 62, Median = 67.5, Mode = none, Range = 94

10. Mean = 64, Median = 75.5, Mode = none, Range = 75

11. Mean = 53.571, Median = 46, Mode = none, Range = 84

12. Mean = 48.714, Median = 48, Mode = none, Range = 83

13. Mean = 51, Median = 51, Mode = none, Range = 67

14. Mean = 45.833, Median = 38.5, Mode = none, Range = 68

15. Mean = 45.571, Median = 43, Mode = none, Range = 48

16. Mean = 60.667, Median = 76.5, Mode = none, Range = 85

17. Mean = 66.167, Median = 76, Mode = none, Range = 74

18. Mean = 30.286, Median = 21, Mode = none, Range = 76

19. Mean = 44.857, Median = 44, Mode = none, Range = 59

20. Mean = 52.714, Median = 54, Mode = none, Range = 69

21. Mean = 64.143, Median = 71, Mode = none, Range = 77

22. Mean = 40.667, Median = 41.5, Mode = none, Range = 91

23. Mean = 41, Median = 48, Mode = none, Range = 84

24. Mean = 50.5, Median = 65.5, Mode = 70, Range = 67

Made in the USA
Columbia, SC
10 July 2024

38432328R00067